CLIFFE
in Old Photographs

By Allan Cherry

Published by Meresborough Books

Cliffe at Hoo Rectory.

INTRODUCTION

Cliffe in former times was much larger than it is today. But in 1520 a fire broke out which spread rapidly, since the houses were timber-framed and tarred, and built close together. There were no fire appliances then, so a large part of medieval Cliffe was burned to the ground.

Cliffe came to life again in 1868 when a cement factory was built down at the creek. The quality of the cement was so good that it was used in the construction of some of the lighthouses around the country, including Eddystone, the Lizard and the Needles.

In 1887 the village had eleven shops. These were a Saddler, a Dressmaker, a Carpenter, two Butchers, three Bakers, a Shoemaker, a Blacksmith and a Watchmaker.

About one hundred years ago, the wage of the workers was around fourteen to eighteen shillings per week for a seventy hour week. Most of the workers remained employed until they were in their seventies, because there was no Old Age Pension until 1909, when five shillings per week was given to any man or woman over the age of seventy.

These photographs are of the old Parish of Cliffe, which covers the area between Merryboys Road, Cooling Street, Buckland Road and the Marshes. Since these photographs were taken, the number of shops in the village has decreased. This book shows the changes in Cliffe over the past one hundred years or so. I have also incorporated some of the people who were born, lived and worked in the village.

The Parish of Cliffe is about five miles from north to south, although just over half of this is marshland. The northern boundary reaches the River Thames, whilst the southern boundary reaches Mortimers.

ACKNOWLEDGEMENTS

I would like to express my thanks to:
Mr F. Martin
Mr H. Knight (late)
Mr J. Filmer
Mr J. Sullivan
Mr R. Hutchings (late)
Mrs D. Milton
'The Chatham News and Standard'

My special thanks to:
Mrs P. Leviston
Mr G. Cherry
Mr R. Millington
Mr P. Hutchings

I would also like to thank friends of the village, who also supplied me with photographs.

Published by Meresborough Books, 17 Station Road, Rainham, Kent. ME8 7RS.

ISBN 0948193 62X

Printed by Headley Brothers Ltd, Ashford, Kent.

Looking up Reed Street from the corner of Wharf Lane. The old wooden houses on the left are where Holmsdale Cottages now stand. They were built in 1884.

Reed Street, with the dusty old road, taken from the corner of Green Lane, where an old walnut tree once stood. The wooden house on the left with a bay window was once a butcher's shop. The shop displaying the 'Lyons Tea' sign was Sacre's, grocery and hardware store.

The Compasses public house in Marsh Lane, which was nicknamed 'The Porters Shop' because the publican, or beer house keeper as he was called in those days, sold Porters Ales.

In 1861 the beer house keeper was William Seamark, who was also a shepherd. He was born at Cliffe and lived in the Compasses with his wife Sarah, who was born at Upnor. They had three daughters, Mary, Eliza and Francis, and two sons, George and John. The eldest daughter, Mary, was a servant. The Compasses was closed down towards the earlier part of this century and is now a private dwelling.

Looking down Reed Street, with Cambrian Terrace, built in 1897, on the right. On the left is a row of shops called 'The Market Place', which included a grocer's and general store, butcher's, dressmaker's, chemist and a sweet shop.

Roasting an ox, circa 1898, down Reed Street, opposite the grocer's store, on the ground known as 'The Green', which is now a car park.

St Helen's Pond, at the bottom of Pond Hill, which was part of the High Street, with Court-sole Farm and the church in the background. Circa 1909. The pond was gradually filled in with rubbish, as there were no collections in those days. The site is now overgrown.

Looking up the High Street, from the top of Pond Hill, with the Black Bull on the left. On the right, with a bicycle wheel hanging up outside, is Bentleys shop.

The Black Bull public house, when it was made of wood. This was pulled down and re-built of brick in 1887. To the left are Miskin Cottages, where Mr Brown, the publican of the Black Bull, built his shop, joining it onto the end of the cottages.

Facing down the High Street, you can see S.A. Brown's shop. This shop had two rooms: the one on the left sold sweets, and on the right was a barber's shop. After Mr Brown died the barber's shop was used once a week by a travelling dentist.

Bentley's cycle shop and newsagents, taken from Soapsuds Alley, incorporating Stockers Gate. A team of four horses, with wagon, took the villagers on outings and was also the main means of transport before cycles came into use.

Looking down the end of the High Street, now Pond Hill. At the bottom of the hill, on the first marsh, was Mr Bowles' yard, where he kept cattle and a couple of horses.

Chicago House, circa 1910, was built in 1893 and had two wooden houses joined onto it. This was originally a shop, hence the large windows at the front.

The butcher's shop in the High Street was run for generations by the Elford family. To the left of the shop was the slaughterhouse, also run by Mr Elford. Circa 1911.

Circa 1911. The Victoria Inn public house. The left hand side of the pub was a greengrocer's shop. Both were run by Mr Thorndike. At the back of the premises was a coalyard.

The view below is taken from almost the same spot nearly half a century earlier. Then the Victoria Inn was known as the Victory. The name was changed when it was rebuilt. At the time of the 1861 census Martha Parker, born in Gillingham in 1814, was listed as 'beer house keeper'. She was a widow with a daughter, Alice, 17, and a son, Thomas, 15, who both worked in the beer house.

Looking down the High Street, circa 1865. Chesterton's grocery and provisions store was also the Post Office at the time. Before becoming a shop there is reason to believe this might have been a beer house, for there are cellar doors outside on the pavement. Before that the site was supposedly four farm cottages. It is now Wilkies restaurant and is a listed building.

Next was the Victory public house, then further down was the old Bakery, which is a listed building. This was built in the early 19th century. Charles Terry was the miller and baker; he was deaf and ran the shop with his wife Sarah. They had three daughters, Julia, Emma and Fanny, and a son, George. Julia, the eldest daughter, was an assistant in the baker's shop.

Then came Longford House, where Joseph and Fanny Mayhew lived. They were both watchmakers. This house was built in the 17th century and has substantial evidence of timber framing. Earlier this century it was the Post Office and Telephone Exchange run by Chestertons. It too is a listed building.

Then came Priors Hall, the other side of Soapsuds Alley, where John and Ann Phipps lived with their three daughters, Mary, Sarah and Charlotte. John was a labourer.

Lastly, at the bottom of the High Street, was the Black Bull public house. It was made of wood and supposedly built on the site of an old graveyard. The cellars beneath the Black Bull are supposed to be haunted.

Circa 1887. The old wooden houses on the left were on the site of the present Lime Tree Villas and Post Office. These houses were owned by the church and used to house the poor.

Circa 1911. The High Street, showing the harness maker's shop, run by Mr Swannell. To the left of Swannell's shop is School House, which John Browne gave by Will in 1679. It was rebuilt in 1868. To the right of Swannell's were three wooden houses, now the village green. On the left of the picture is the Six Bells Inn. The man in the doorway is probably the landlord, W.J. Thorndike. Was he any relation of Dame Sybil and Russell Thorndike who grew up in Rochester, their father being attached to the Cathedral from 1884 on?

Mr Swannell outside his shop, holding a horse's collar, which would have been hand made. He would have had to measure the horse himself, so that when the collar was finished it would fit perfectly. A badly fitting collar would rub the horse, as it was worn all day in the fields. Mr Swannell would not just make harnesses, he would make or repair anything to do with leather. One of his jobs would be to mend the leather bellows across the road at the forge. He would also sew buckles back onto the children's shoes, as they sat on his workbench, watching. One of the devices used by the harness maker was called a clam. He would sit on a low stool and hold this wooden device between his knees. It was a type of clamp or vice that held the leather tight, so he had both hands free to work with. The harness maker usually sewed with two needles, each of which came from opposite sides of his work. Swannell's sold a host of items, including brass cleaner for the buckles and horse brasses, oil for the horses' hooves, saddle soap to soften the leather and grooming brushes, in fact, anything to do with horses that he was able to get into the shop.

The Six Bells Inn. Circa 1911, showing the horses and wagon loaded up with the villagers, all ready for an afternoon's outing. To the left behind the railings is the forge, where the horses were taken to be shod. Farming implements were also taken to the forge to be repaired.

St Helen's School was a National Church School and was built in three stages. The first part of the school was built in 1854 and the last stage in 1879. Before this was built the school was held in a hall, next to the Methodist Church.

The first village taxi, taken outside St Helen's School. The car, a Model T Ford, was owned and run by Norman Thorpe, whose father was the publican at the Six Bells Inn. The school is now turned into private dwellings.

St Helen's Cottages, at the top of the Buttway, were named after the village church. The houses face Buttway Lane and back onto the graveyard.

Circa 1920. St Helen's Church. The church was built circa 1260. It is dedicated in honour of St Helen, mother of the Emperor Constantine the Great. The oldest parts of the church are the Tower, Transepts and Nave, which date back to the 13th century.

There used to be only six bells in the belfry until two more were added in 1864. These were cast in the foundry of John Taylor & Co., Loughborough. There is a single room above the porch, called a 'parvise' (priests room) or treasury. It has a fireplace, probably from when it was used as a schoolroom for the children of the parish.

The churchyard is very large, approximately two acres in extent. The roof of the church is steep, this is how it was when it was first built, then about 1730 the roof was lowered to give it just a slight slope, then towards the latter part of the last century it was raised again.

The East window, above the Altar, was renewed in 1884 and the North Aisle and Nave were restored. In 1897, at a cost of £4,000, the church was restored.

The church is built of ragstone and flint in alternate layers and is on the site of a wooden Saxon church, dating back to 774. In the foreground is the Buttway, where archery practice took place on Sunday mornings after the church service.

Mr Elford, the butcher from the High Street, in his younger days, on his rounds, delivering meat to the customers in Buttway Lane. Circa 1911. The houses in the background are Kangaroo Villas, built in 1904.

Inside St Helen's Church, looking east up the aisle towards the Altar and Choir Stalls. To the right, behind the pillars, the organ pipes can be seen. Medieval markings on some of the pillars are prominent. The pulpit stands on a stone base at the North East corner of the Nave, the roof of which was destroyed in 1730. At the western end of the church is the choir vestry.

The Chancel has six ancient windows which are arranged in pairs, two of Kentish tracery and the other four of Flamboyant. The steps to the Chancel were destroyed and some parcloses removed about 1640. In 1869 the Chancel steps were replaced and the floor paved with tiles. In 1875 the East wall of the Chancel was examined and traces of the reredos of the ancient Altar were found. It was five feet high by seven feet six inches wide, and had a low pediment.

Circa 1909. The fun corner at the annual sports day, which was held in a field at the back of Manor Farm. Horse jumping and pony trotting were some of the main attractions.

Circa 1910. The hurdle race, at the annual sports day. The chimneys in the background are those of the recently built cement factory at Black Lane.

Circa 1916. Looking down Buttway Lane. To the right of the trees was the sports field. Further down was the old fire station. On the left are St Helen's Cottages.

Manor Farm, at West Street, was built in the late 16th century. It is timber framed with plaster infilling. The cellar is made entirely of brick and has many archways and a drain. Circa 1904.

Circa 1905. A fire at Manor farmhouse practically gutted the house. The firemen with their old pumps fought in vain to save the house from total destruction. Villagers gathered to watch the blaze, while a policeman stood guard inside the farm gates.

Once the fire at Manor farmhouse was extinguished, the extent of the damage could be seen. In those days all the firemen were volunteers. Apart from the chimneys, all that was left standing were the north facing rooms and the kitchen.

The Co-op outing to the hopfields, which the workers enjoyed every year. In the background is Quickrills farmhouse which was built in the early 18th century, and still stands.

The store was divided into three shops. The right for grocery and provisions. To the left was a butcher's and in the middle was a drapery. The Co-op also delivered oil and coal.

Inside the store was an aerial railway, where any payment to be made from one of the counters was placed in the cup, accompanied by the bill. A wire was pulled by the sales person and the cash was sent hurtling across the shop to the cashier's office. Any change would be sent back by the same method, with a dividend voucher included.

The Co-operative movement was run by a local committee, and was an asset to the villagers. At one point in time, the dividend paid was half a crown for every pound spent in the shop. This was a great help to the poor people of the village.

The advantage of dealing with the Co-operative Society was that, after paying working expenses and five per cent interest on Share Capital, the whole of the remaining profits were shared by the members, according to the proportion of their purchases. Non members were entitled to half Members' Dividend. Any person could become a member by paying one shilling for a Share Book and Rules. Forms of application and information were obtainable at the store.

D.G. Knowles was a bootmaker and leather seller. The old black wooden shop had its accommodation behind and above the workshop. It stood on the site of the present fish shop.

Spion Kop Cottages got their name from the area known as Spion Kop, at the bottom of Allens Hill. They were situated to the right of the Co-op, and their walls were two feet thick. The Waghorn sisters lived there, where they ran the village laundry. Circa 1908.

Circa 1910. The Methodist Church once stood to the right of the Temperance Club. Behind it stood the church hall, much used for wedding receptions and parties.

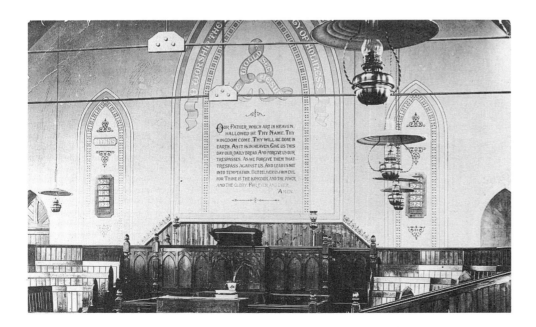

Inside the Methodist Church. The two doors at the back of the church led out to the hall, which stood separate from the church itself. Later on, an organ was installed, which covered the door on the right. The church was lit by paraffin lamps.

Looking up the High Street, showing Longford House when it used to be the old Post Office.

Station Road, circa 1908, now called Church Street, showing the Malthouse and Knowles the bootmakers on the left, and Spion Kop Cottages and the Co-op on the right.

Church Street. The Evening Star public house, where the doors opened directly on to the main road. To the right, adjoining the pub, were three wooden houses. Their site is now a car park.

Station Road, before 1909. To the left, the sweet shop and Evening Star, and on the right, the first two houses of Violet Cottages, built in 1899. The rest of the cottages were not added until a later date, owing to financial difficulties.

Weekes, the butcher's shop, was on the corner of Church Street and Turner Street. Now a private house adjoining the wool shop. Sid Weekes is the second from the right.

Corn once grew where the present tennis courts and sports field are. The sheaves of corn were stood on end. About eight sheaves propped each other up, this was called 'Shocking Up'. It was done to dry out the corn and straw.

Over the years the bowling green has not altered a lot, except that at one time it was surrounded by a tall privet hedge. The old shed has been demolished and a clubhouse erected in its place.

Chatsworth House, May Cottages and St Helen's Terrace, taken before Norwood Corner School was built in 1907. May Cottages got their name because every house in the row had a May tree planted in the front garden.

The Globe Cinema was erected in 1921 on the corner of Higham Road and Church Street. Originally it had been an old government building. It was opened on August Bank Holiday, showing the film 'Ivanhoe', with seating for 300 people. It was put up for sale in 1965, then demolished.

Taken before 1912, Norwood Road, now called Cooling Road, looking from the Norwood Corner crossroads. Norwood Cottages, on the left, were built in 1868. On the right were open fields.

Looking towards the crossroads, from Norwood Road. Once open fields on the left, these houses were built in 1914 for the staff that worked at the Curtis and Harvey powder works.

Norwood Road, Cliffe.

Station Road, circa 1912, looking towards the village. The houses known as The Crescent had not yet been built, opposite Simmonds's Hole. The house on the left, called 'Curhar', was named from the first three letters of Curtis and Harvey, and was built for the manager to live in.

Station Road, Cliffe.

16

Circa 1912. South View was known as the 'Soldiers Rest'. Made from corrugated tin, it was a canteen for the troops serving in the First World War. It was situated at the top of Symonds Road, in Higham Road. Entertainment was put on for the troops in the evenings.

An aerial view of the village. At the bottom right hand corner is Swingate Farm, where Swingate Avenue got its name from. It was situated on the site of the present Swingate Avenue and Quickrills Avenue intersection. The cornfield, known as Glebe Meadow, behind the houses (top right), is now Church Close.

Ben Johnson harvesting with a team of three horses in his field at the bottom of North Road. This field is now an extension to the orginal North Road and covered in houses.

Circa 1913. Taken from the present sports field, Town Road, now called Church Street, with Beslees sweet shop to the left of St Helen's Terrace. Next to that is Polly Ward's hardware shop (which later became Smith's hardware store), and to the left is Norwood School.

This is the back view of Little West Court Farm, a thatched house in Salt Lane, on the corner of the roadway leading to West Court Farm. The ground is now a Tree Surgeon's yard. The lane led to the salt pans on Higham Marshes, hence the name Salt Lane.

Approaching the Nine Elms cement factory, owned by Francis & Co., on the Creek Road. Opened in 1868, Cliffe was the first place in Kent to manufacture cement. The cement was exported by sea from the creek. When the factory opened, the chalk from Black Lane, a mile away, was transported by barges, on a canal that ran from Black Lane to the creek, close to the Canal Tavern public house.

In the early 1870s permission was granted by Lord Darnley to build a tramway, as the factory expanded. The barges and canal were too primitive to cope with the influx of chalk needed at the whitening works. The tramway was constructed to a gauge of 3′8½″ and was a single track on practically flat ground, and the line was almost straight. In the quarry there were many sidings, which splayed out, and a couple of them went into the clay pits.

When the barges came into the works at the creek, they brought with them coke which was sent up to the kilns in the quarry in the empty wagons. Running parallel with the 'main line' was a single track that ran from the whitening works to the quarry, alongside the disused canal. This line was joined to the main line by a short spur, at the western end. About 1900 the Francis Company was taken over by the British Portland Cement Co.

This factory closed in 1921.

Marsh House was on the right hand side, going down the Creek Road, towards the old Francis & Co. cement works.

Outside the Three Merry Boys public house, circa 1914. This pub was quite popular because it was the only one at Cliffe Woods.

This was the second cement factory to be built at Cliffe. It was next to the present Oil Storage Company, along Black Lane, known locally as 'The Track'.

The Royal Albert public house, with Concrete Cottages built in 1878 to the right and Cliff Ville to the left. Concrete Cottages still stand along with the Royal Albert, whilst Cliff Ville was demolished many years ago, to make room for the factory silos.

The demolition of one of the factory chimneys at the Black Lane works, owned by Francis & Co.

A third cement factory was built at Cliffe, in Salt Lane. Its silos were 112 feet high, and the tallest chimney was a little over 200 feet. The factory produced approximately 1,000 tons of cement a day.

The loco train at the front of the cement factory at Salt Lane was loaded up with cement and taken down to the jetty, to be shipped away. The factory closed in 1970. The two chimneys were blown up in December 1979 and the silos in March 1980.

The old iron loco train ran from the Black Lane cliffs, where the wagons were loaded up with chalk, and it pulled them down to the whitening works at the creek. Each night the engine was housed in a shed at Black Lane.

A ship tied up at Alpha Jetty, Cliffe, situated on the River Thames. The Stothert and Pitt cranes, that were used to load the cement onto the ships, tower above it.

The Coastguard houses are situated on the marshes, next to the River Thames. They can be reached via the 'Hope Point Road'. There are seven houses in the row, and the one on the far left was lived in by the Coastguard.

Fruit pickers in the orchard at Hornes Farm, Perry Hill. The women would fill their large baskets, then carry them to where the men would pack them into more shallow but wider baskets.

The Charnel House, in the north west corner of the churchyard, was built in the mid 19th century. It was used as a mortuary for the bodies that were found in the River Thames, until such time that they were buried.

Workmen in Hornes Orchard, with the baskets that the fruit was packed into. Over the top of the fruit a printed piece of paper was placed, quoting, 'W. Horne & Sons, Fruit Growers, Cliffe, Kent'. The baskets were then taken to the railway station, for transportation to the markets.

The Hope Point Road runs from the end of Pickles Way to the Lower Hope Point. Now there are lakes on the left that were dug to get chalk for the cement factory.

Circa 1908. The Beehive public house was in Cooling Street, to the south of the present Staff of Life public house. This thatched beerhouse was somewhat unusual, due to its being round.

A token depicting 'Cliffe 1^d Schools'. Red House, in Reed Street, was once one of these private schools, where the children were sent, at the cost of one old penny per week.

Rye Street, with the farm entrance on the left, next to the white farmhouse. Now the only old houses left in Rye Street are the farthest two on the left. Circa 1912.

Children outside the National Church School of St Helen's. Circa 1890.

The white farmhouse at the entrance to the farm at Rye Street, after a Stirling Bomber crashed into it in October 1942, killing a woman inside, but missing the thatched barn on the right, which contained 40 cows.

Berry Court, once known as Burye-court, was land belonging to the crown. Henry VIII granted the manor of Burye-court and land that belonged to it to Sir George Brooke, who was Lord Cobham, at a yearly rent of £7.13s.8½d.

His grandson, Henry Lord Cobham, through conviction of high treason, was deprived of his rights to the estate, so it had to be forfeited to the crown. The estate was then granted to Sir Robert Cecil, Earl of Salisbury, later Lord Treasurer of England, who was married to Elizabeth, the sister of Henry Lord Cobham. He passed it to Bernard Hyde Esq. Many generations later one of his descendants sold it to Mr Harvey whose son, Samuel Clay Harvey, died possessed of it in 1791.

Since then this land has been divided up and sold many times.

Circa 1912. Leonard Dowsett with pony, at the gateway to Rye Street. He became a shepherd and managed a flock of sheep on the priory marshes at Cliffe.

The Marshes, circa 1918. The trees in the distance were to hide the Curtis and Harvey powder works. On the marshes during the Second World War there were two schemes to divert the German planes from bombing Gravesend and Rochester airports. The first was a flare path that was near Boatwick House, where the shepherd lived. Most people know Boatwick House as the old Dutch barn, on the Hope Point Road. Close to the house a shelter was built for the aircraftmen, but this project was soon abandoned. Then a second project was brought in, a dummy airfield, by which a bunker was built near the Fleet. There was a generator close to the bunker for powering the lights of the (never-built) landing strip. To attract the incoming German bombers, the lights of the dummy airfield all faced east, with the exception of the occasional floodlamps on top of the bunker.

Four aircraftmen at one time had billets in the village and took turns to operate the decoy lights.

On the decayed jetties of the old explosives works at Hope Point, more lights were fixed and were switched on to persuade the Germans that the zone was a suitable target.

There were many parachuted mines and bombs dropped and Mr Jack Robertson, the Chief Air Raid Warden, tried to count systematically. His total for this parish was 736 bombs.

Thatched roofs on the straw stacks were a common sight. It was done to keep the straw dry. This thatcher was working on Baldock's farm.

Mr Sturt, the owner of the butcher's shop in Read Street, is holding the steer that he purchased after it had won third prize at a show.

Cliffe football team 1908-9, outside the church gates. If any away matches were to be played, the team would be transported by a horse drawn coach.

Cliffe Scouts' football team. Circa 1918. Taken on the recreation ground, up Buttway Lane.

Cliffe Scouts' football team 1920-21, with the local Coastguard, Mr Pearman (back left).

This group of locals is standing round a tiny crater made by a bomb on Christmas Day 1914.

In the distance the drone of an aeroplane engine was heard, coming from the east. It was a German mono plane. Guns from all directions opened fire as the plane passed over Kingsnorth and Cliffe, heading in the direction of London. It came under fire from a multitude of guns at Chattenden, Upnor and the Lower Hope Point at Cliffe. It may have been there to try to destroy the gunpowder works at Kingsnorth and Cliffe. Soon there was peace again, but not for long, as the plane returned within an hour, and in hot pursuit was a British fighter from Dartford. With shrapnel falling from the local guns, this did not deter the villagers from standing in the streets, watching.

This event was the first aerial 'dog fight' ever to take place in Kent. A metal object fell from the German plane and this turned out to be an eighteen pound bomb that fell at the top of Blue Gates Hill, known as Whites Hill.

Cliffe was the first village in Kent to be bombed.

Evidence suggests that the German bomber was destroyed.

Blue Gates Hill is situated at the south of the parish on the main road from Cliffe to the Medway Towns. At the bottom of the hill is Mortimer's farm. Hugh de Mortimer was the owner of the estate during the reign of Edward III. Later it was owned by the Englesfeild family, supposedly of Saxon extraction. Sir Thomas Englesfeild was the Speaker of the House of Commons during the reign of Henry VII.

Later it was sold to Mr Thomas Polley, then sold again to Robert Lee by Polley's great grandson, George Polley. Robert Lee's son, William, was surveyor of the navy during the reign of Queen Anne. He was twice married, firstly to Samuel Pett's daughter, Elizabeth, then to Catherine, daughter of William Johnson. William Lee died in 1757 and left much of the estate to his kinswoman, Mrs Ward, with remainder to her brother, Rear Admiral Henry Ward. On the death of Henry Ward, about 1768, it was left to his son Edward Vernon Ward.

Since this time the property has changed hands many times and is now occupied by Frederick White.

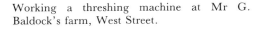
Working a threshing machine at Mr G. Baldock's farm, West Street.

Cliffe fire brigade were the winners of the Webb Cup at 'Ye Olde St Barts Fayre', July 21st-24th 1919. This photograph was taken in the garden of the old chemist's shop, Church Street.

At a meeting of councillors on 9th September 1901 in the Cliffe Schools, the chairman pointed out that it was the duty of the Council to call a parish meeting of the whole of the parish under the Lighting and Watching Act of 1833, asking them to grant a sum of money to cover the cost of buying necessary fire appliances for the village.

After another meeting on 30th September 1901 it was said that the amount needed to purchase a Merryweather Pump would be between £300 and £350.

Shortly after, the necessary money was obtained and a Merryweather Pump was purchased. These pumps were pulled by horses, so if there was a fire, the first person to hear about it would run to the marshes and fetch the horses up to the fire station at Buttway Lane, which no longer exists. The horses were then hitched to the pump before setting off to the fire.

This photograph shows the old fire station still in use to house a post war appliance. By this time responsibility for fire fighting had passed from the parish council to Kent Fire Brigade.

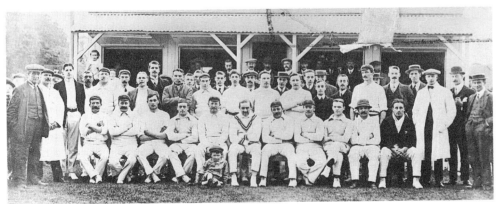

The Curtis and Harvey cricket team versus the village team, 1919.

Curtis and Harvey powder works were proposed in 1901. They were built at Redham Mead and covered an area of 60 acres. When the factory was in full production it employed about 2,000 people. The storage areas were surrounded by walls of earth, in case of an explosion.

Most of the workers were transported to and from the Medway towns by a coach, pulled by six horses. Then in about 1914 bicycles with pneumatic tyres were in general use, so any worker could purchase one from the Curtis and Harvey system of hire purchase. Each week the worker was stopped so much from his wage until the cycle was paid for in full. Then in about 1915 the first motor cars to be seen in the village were at Curtis and Harveys.

The works were constructed for storage, so the term 'factory' is somewhat of a misnomer. The works had two jetties on the River Thames and a 2ft gauge railway track, probably made of wood, to lessen the sparks, was used to link various parts of the works. The works closed in 1921. During the works' twenty years existence there were sixteen deaths caused by explosions.

The rear view of the old Rectory, once known as Priors Hall. During the Saxon period, around AD600, the area of the old Rectory was settled by monks, and in 774 a royal charter gave land close by to the Archbishop of Canterbury. At this time Bromhege was the name given to all of Cliffe and Cooling.

The Archbishop and the monks built a residence which was kept until 1195 by subsequent Archbishops. It was then known as Priors Hall. In 1337 the Bishop of Rochester rebuilt Priors Hall at some considerable cost.

Up until the beginning of the 19th century the house was leased to numerous laymen, then in 1869 it was rebuilt as a Rectory, when the Reverend Henry Lloyd was the rector in residence. In 1880 the rector's income was £1,097 per year, an enormous amount for those days. Remains of the original building still stand and an original doorway still exists at the rear of the building. At the front of the old Rectory you can see clearly the remains of an ancient buttress.

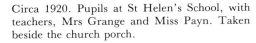

Circa 1920. Pupils at St Helen's School, with teachers, Mrs Grange and Miss Payn. Taken beside the church porch.

Cliffe railway station and station master's house, taken from Station Approach. The station building consisted of a porters' room and storeroom, booking office, parcel room, lobby and toilets, and was made of wooden clapboard. The signal box was on the down side of the tracks. On the opening day of the line the station was decorated with bunting and many villagers gathered to cheer as the first train rolled into Cliffe from Gravesend, decked with flags. This was a 'guest' train, packed with ladies and gentlemen. After a short stop the train proceeded on its way to Sharnal Street.

The station had a small goods yard to the east side. Goods handled at Cliffe included grain, milk and fruit. The cement industry did not use the line until 1961.

The Canal Tavern public house, nicknamed The Shant, was at the top end of the creek and run by Mr and Mrs Else (pictured). Apart from drink, they sold groceries and provisions to the men who came into the Nine Elms cement works with their barges.

Cliffe Territorial Army in 1911. The Territorials were a British Army of Home Defence, instituted on a local basis in 1908, and consisted of men living at home and doing occasional periods of drill and other training.

The Three Merry Boys public house, at Cooling Common, which is now called Merryboys Road. Standing in the doorway (far left) is Mr Potter, the landlord. Circa 1916.

Cliffe railway station had its first passenger train in March 1882. It ran from Gravesend to Sharnal Street. The fruit baskets on the platform are from Horne's farm. The station closed for passengers in November 1960. Circa 1910.

A balloon that came down in a field near Rye Street. Circa 1924.

Children at Norwood Corner School, with teacher Miss Elford. Some of the children are wearing medals that were given out each year along with a certificate for perfect attendance. The medals were not given after 1919.

Dressed as Pearly King and Queen for the village carnival, Elsie and Bill Comfort on the Wellpenn Road. Circa 1915.

Polly Ward's shop, opposite the present tennis courts, sold provisions and hardware. She also gave piano lessons. Before that her father, Mr Hughes, had it as a furniture showroom, and at the rear of the house was a large building he had as a cabinet makers' and joiners' shop.

Cooling Street School, built in 1908, is now a private dwelling. It is situated south of the present Staff of Life public house.

Buckland Road, circa 1912, looking towards the village, with the farm entrance on the left. The black houses no longer exist, but behind them, still standing, is a 17th century barn and wagon porch, which is a listed building.

Mr W.H. Slater on his land yacht, 1938. Known as 'Tubby Slater', he constructed his yacht from a cement tipping truck, with boards for the deck, a soap box to sit on and ordinary sheets for the sails.

The old cricket pavilion on the marsh at the bottom of Pond Hill, when it used to be a sports field. Once a year, in the summer, 'Penfolds Travelling Fair' used to come to the village and use the same sports field, to provide entertainment for a few days.

Outside West Court Farm. The First Cliffe Parish Council 1894-96. Left to right, back row: C. Knight, W. Jarrett, W. Randall, A.L. Chesterton, J. Smith, H. Wilden.

Front row: W. Woolley, S. Hammond (vice chairman), Frederick Wright (chairman), A.E. Grubb (clerk), C. Lake.

The Victoria Inn public house, when it was run by Mr Thorndike. The room nearest the bakery was used as a greengrocer's.

Cliffe Fort was built in 1860 under the supervision of General Charles Gordon. General Gordon was born in 1833, and at the age of fifteen started his army career as an officer cadet. In 1852 he passed out of the Royal Engineers as a Second Lieutenant. General Gordon was murdered in the Palace of Khartoum, in January 1885.

In 1871 General Gordon wrote to the Francis & Co. cement works, complaining that the fumes from the works' kilns were injurious to the health of the soldiers that were stationed in the fort and demanded action should be taken immediately. The staff of the works had an iron chimney built in sections, so that when it was erected it was tall enough to allow the smoke to go way above the fort.

In 1866 the fort was an experimental station for the Brennan Torpedo and the torpedo was installed at the fort to hit vessels as they went up the river. The torpedo was invented by an Irish-born Australian named Louis Brennan. The War Office adopted the torpedo as a harbour defence weapon in 1887. The two launching bays and rails for the launching still remain at the west side of the fort.

When the fort was built, the guns installed were 68 pounders, smooth bore, that had a range of about 3,000 yards, but against armoured vessels this gun was no good, so in 1874 they were replaced by enormous guns weighing up to 38 tons. These were heavy rifled muzzle-loading guns in casements, traversed on metal rails.

Around 1905 the heavy guns were replaced by light and medium guns and 4 x 12-pdr quick firing guns were added.

The inside of the fort, which was last used during the Second World War, was re-armed with two 4″ guns for close defence. The fort was manned mainly by the Home Guard and a few regulars.

The Victoria Inn had an annual outing to the hopfields on a Saturday afternoon for many years. In this picture it is horse drawn wagons that are ready to set off on a hopping outing. The wagons, although open, had a sheet of canvas rolled up on top, in case of bad weather.

This picture shows a dramatic change in transport but remarkably little change in the men's dress. The Maidstone and District charabancs were not comfortable to ride in with their transverse benches. Some of the earlier charabancs had solid tyres. This vehicle is a 1930 Leyland Tiger KR7404.

Bentley's shop, in the High Street, sold a variety of things, ranging from newspapers and cards to china, toys and bicycles. Now this site is the post office and private accommodation. On the far left are Lime Tree Cottages.

This aeroplane was in trouble and had to make an emergency landing in a field at Salt Lane (south side), where there is now a disused quarry. After the plane was mended the pilot gave rides, for a price.

Courtsole farmhouse, a listed building, was built in the 16th century with some 18th century additions. The property of the Ropers for some generations, until Christopher Roper (Lord Teynham), transferred the ownership in 1645 to Sir Edward Monins. The Filmers now reside there.

This orchard was at the back of Courtsole Farm and ran along to 'The Pickle'. The near side of the orchard now has farm buildings on it, since the trees were grubbed out some decades ago. The rest of the land is arable.

The overhead wires with buckets attached carried coal, brought in barges to the jetty that was near the fort, to the cement factory in Salt Lane, to fuel the kilns. All that remains of the jetty is the wooden piles.

The creek bungalow was at first owned by the Nine Elms cement company. Looking from the river, it lay on the right of the factory buildings. It was originally built for one of the managers. The bungalow remained occupied for many years after the factory was demolished.

Black Path is about three feet wide and runs from the top of Allens Hill to the entrance to the picnic grounds, at Black Lane.

Turner Street was built by the Francis & Co. cement works to house some of its workers. The Street got its name from the first manager at the works, Mr Turner.

To the south side of Turner Street is Millcroft Road, which got its name from the windmill that once stood there, on the site of the present Prospect Cottages, built in 1888. This Black Smock Mill killed a boy from Frindsbury, by the name of Pope, when one of the sweeps (sails) hit him. These sweeps almost touched the ground. The Smock Mill had the main body built of wood on top of a brick base. The mill stood idle for a number of years without its sweeps until it was burnt down about 1885.

This is the site of the present Cliffe Surgery. St George's Villas, with bay windows, had Ashby's sweet shop on the end, at the corner of Turner Street. The half wooden houses were Wellington Place, which had a hat shop on the end, at the corner of Millcroft Road.

Circa 1930. Some of the charabancs had soft tops that folded back like a concertina. There was always one charabanc that was for men only, and that one especially had plenty of beer on board. These hopping outings were mainly to Paddock Wood and Tonbridge. This vehicle, KP3024, was made in Maidstone by Tilling-Stevens in 1928.

Circa 1907. Canon H.B. Boyd on his bicycle, along Cooling Common. The lamp on his bicycle had carbide put into it, then set alight, to produce a light.

Circa 1907. Canon H.B. Boyd outside the North Door of St Helen's Church. A bachelor, he became rector at Cliffe in 1899.

The Lady Chapel, also known as the North Transept, has the largest stained glass window in the church. There is a smaller window here depicting St Helen. This is where the rectors held ecclesiastical meetings up until the mid 19th century.

A view of Cliffe from the church tower, looking east. On the far left is Wharf Farm, which was built in the 18th century at the bottom of Wharf Lane. This was named from the creeks and inlets that spurred from the River Thames and was the site of a wharf where smuggling took place. It is said that in medieval times the waters of the river came up to the foot of the cliffs at the bottom of Allens Hill.

In the centre is Reed Street, where there were numerous shops and businesses. Two thirds of the way down Reed Street on the left hand side was 'Reeves', the builder's yard. Walter Reeves had a thriving business. His trades included: builder, wheelwright, decorator, plumber, glazier and undertaker. Reeves made coffins in the upper room of his workshop, sometimes working late into the night. When Reeves moved away from the village the business was taken over by Norman Savage.

On the south side of Reed Street was the Plymouth Brethren Chapel, and when the Plymouth Brethren moved away from Cliffe, Norman Savage used the chapel as a carpenter's workshop.

Many carpenters have lived in Cliffe, including Richard Chicheley, who carved the figurehead of Lord Nelson's ship 'The Victory'.

Another builder, decorator and undertaker in the village was C.B. Hughes of Higham Road. In 1931 his charge to supply a polished elm coffin with brass trimmings, conveying deceased from Rochester Hospital to Cliffe and attendance, tolling bell, burial fees, four bearers, hearse, two horse drawn coaches and drivers, came to £11.12s.6d.

St Helen's Church, when the roof was leaded and had only a slight gradient. On top of the porch was a small brick and wood building, containing a stairway to the porch roof. The gates were wooden and carved at the top. Before 1879.

1925. A motorbike and sidecar in the High Street. Longford House is to the right, which is a listed building, and Priors Hall to the left, which was at one time a shoe repairers, until it was demolished in 1934. Between them is Soapsuds Alley.

Handbell ringers, outside St Helen's Church. Circa 1925.

The presentation of a cup at a shearing match, 1912, in the field at the back of Courtsole Farm, that runs parallel with Pickles Way.

40

Joyce's butcher's shop, in the Market Place, was the butcher's before Sturts took over. Here, Christmas 1913, they had so much meat that the grocery shop to the left gave permission for it to be displayed outside their shop.

Circa 1910. Looking south across the Buttway can be seen the old forge, the Methodist Church and, in the distance, Turner Street. Taken from the church tower.

1850. Children at play on the Buttway. This was before the last part of the school was built.

41

The Co-op bread cart at the top of Pond Hill. The cart was loaded up at the Co-op, in Station Road, now Church Street, and pushed around the village. The delivery man would park it, and then from that loaded up his bread basket, to deliver it door to door.

Looking up Pond Hill, with Thames Terrace on the right. On the left are two wooden cottages adjoining Chicago House. During the First World War a petrol bomb landed on the side roof of the house nearest to the bottom of the hill.

An artist's impression of the cement works at the creek, from the River Thames.

GENERAL VIEW OF THE NINE ELMS CEMENT WORKS, CLIFFE, KENT.

Circa 1900. Reverend Boyd on far right, with Reverend Walters (third in from left), who was curate and later became vicar of Hoo. The lady who is sitting second from right was Miss Bellamy and she is holding a board that reads 'Guild of Cleaners'.

Standing: Rev. Boyd, Mrs Heard, Mrs Humphreys, Mrs Smith (midwife), Mrs Loft, Mrs Buckman, Mrs Scott (husband an ice skater, who drove his ducks to the pond, daily) and Ewart West (organist, whose wife was the last case of ague).

Seated: Mrs Relph, Miss Bellamy, Mrs Evernden, Mrs Orman. Circa 1910.

A team of horses and wagon in the High Street, in between the Six Bells public house and Swannells, the harness makers. In the background is Parker's shop. Circa 1909.

St Helen's pond. Circa 1910. Looking east. The landway on the right runs to the bottom of Marsh Lane.

Looking down Reed Street, with Red House, a listed building, on the right. This house was built in the early 18th century and has a speaking tube to the left of the door, built into the brickwork. On the left is Amy Terrace, built in 1890.

Red House was the residence of Arthur Boyd Rogers, who was born in 1864 and later became the village doctor. He held his surgery each morning and evening, then in between times, did his rounds, either by walking or on his bicycle. The doctor could be contacted at any time. If it was out of surgery times you could call at his house, day or night. You would ring the bell, then speak into the tube at the door.

Dr Rogers retired in 1944 at the age of 80. His son Andrew became doctor of Cliffe. Now the surgery is in Church Street.

Circa 1914. Cooling Street, with the school on the right, looking north towards the village.

At about the turn of the century there was a band at Cliffe. The wording on the drum reads 'Cliffe at Hoo Brass Band'.

Cliffe takes its name from the cliff on which it stands. On the right is Allens Hill, and below that is Spion Kop. There was once a pond at the bottom of the hill, called Allens Hill Pond.

Circa 1910. This row of shops was called St George's Terrace, and contained four shops. From left to right were: Luckhurst the baker's, Green's general stores, Edge's drapery store and Weeke's the butchers. Luckhurst's were later taken over by Carrington's. Edge's drapery store was where the wool shop is now.

45

Circa 1910. Facing down Pond Hill, with St Helen's Pond at the bottom. To the left is the entrance to Courtsole Farm and on the right is the Glebe meadow. Pickles Way starts at the bottom of the hill.

Aerial view of Baldock's Farm at West Street, with West Street cottages on the left. These cottages were demolished many decades ago.

Berry Court farmhouse. This three storey house once stood to the left of the farmyard opposite Redbarn cottage.

A back view of a house named 'The Rookery'. It once stood in Common Lane, on the south side. It got its name from the trees that surrounded it, that the rooks nested in. Common Lane runs from the bottom of Reed Street to Rye Street.

Newlands Nursery was owned by Victor Weekes who lived in 'Newlands House', now called Almond Lodge. His bulb fields were at Station Road, running from Simmonds's Hole to the present farm shop. He grew tulips, daffodils, hyacinths and gladioli. In the distance are Morning Cross Cottages.

A lorry loaded up with boxes of flowers at Newlands Nursery, ready to take them to Covent Garden. Apart from packing the flowers at the nursery, the women also made wreaths and wedding bouquets. The area was nick-named 'Little Holland'.

Sturts the butchers was in the parade of shops called the Market Place, in Reed Street. Here the wagons are hitched to the horses awaiting the delivery round. To the right of the butcher's was a dressmaker's shop owned by Mr Frayling, who was German.

Circa 1907. The train at Cliffe Station was called a Railmotor. It was built in 1906 with the steam engine and carriage combined as one unit. In 1925 the engine was separated from the Railmotor.

Norwood School was built in 1907 to take the overflow of children from St Helen's School. This school was built on the site of the present Norwood Close.